Mercury

SIMON SMITH's previous books are *Fifteen Exits* (Waterloo Press, 2001) and *Reverdy Road* (Salt Publications, 2003). His translations of Catullus and Pierre Reverdy have appeared in *PN Review* and *Poetry Review*. He was a judge of the Poetry Society's 2004 National Poetry Prize and is librarian of the Poetry Library in London.

Mercury

SIMON SMITH

29.i.09

S
SALT

CAMBRIDGE

PUBLISHED BY SALT PUBLISHING
PO Box 937, Great Wilbraham, Cambridge PDO CB1 5JX United Kingdom

© Simon Smith, 2006

First published 2006

Printed and bound in the United Kingdom by Lightning Source

Typeset in Swift 9.5 / 13

ISBN-10 1 84471 254 0 paperback
ISBN-13 978 1 84471 254 0 paperback

SP

1 3 5 7 9 8 6 4 2

for Flick, always

Contents

Acknowledgments

Angel Exhaust 18 Spring 2005 for "Gum Spots", "Mending Wall", "Language", "Timber", "Radio", "Aide-Memoire", "Cube Moves", "Bet Wit", "Tee Hee", "Of", "Polyester Cotton Mix", "Over the Page".

Cambridge Conference of Contemporary Poetry 12 Review ([Cambridge]: CCCP 2002) for "Meanwhile" and "Second Coat".

Oasis No 106 2002 for "Orpheus", "Rain", and "Twelfth".

Onedit 3, (http://www.onedit.net) for "Simon", "Thin Air", "White", "Shiny Beach", "To Moment", "Pfuff", "Surveillance Camera", "A Harsh Light".

Painted, Spoken number 3 2001 for "Buzz", "Lorca", "Tint".

Poetry Review Volume 92 No 3 Autumn 2002 for "Heaps".

Poetry Review Volume 93 No1 Spring 2003 for "Slips Light", "Day One", "Puts You in the Picture", "Who's Whose", "Reality", "Warm Rain".

"Noir", in *Air-Shaped*, Lyric Editions: Ottawa, 2004, original calligraphy and watercolours by Chan Ky-Yut.

My thanks to those editors, curators and artists: Tim Atkins, Charles Bainbridge, Chan Ky-Yut, Andrew Duncan, David Herd, Rod Mengham, Kevin Nolan, Nicole Presentey, Richard Price, Robert Potts, and Ian Robinson.

Mercury

Buzz

The breeze is the note left by the meadow

For me to read hold it up to the blue

It's Real Life down here, you know

It's all right shooting live ammo

Through my head things go straight

Trapped in a box not the message

Lorca

I want one true word

With you Jack Spicer

Today tomorrow and every other day

I push out on the rise

Angled in to wobble at the ankle

That's not cricket in my base

Ball scores and the breeze drop

It one way today tomorrow

Or any other day no mail for you

[4]

Second Coat

This poem comes with a drawing.

Politics never far from the surface.

Circa sixty-five or sixty-six the trail goes cold.

If I wait long enough I'll see you.

Hands over eyes tight shut.

On the John Updike trail this Fall.

Power by any other name.

Every line ends with a dot or a full-stop

Tint

The past we all disappear into one

Liner or continuous text messaging

It's the refund I stand for welcome

To my path we mean no harm

To your big toe we're not receiving

The buzz mess and tangle

Fame won't show on the print

Licking my lips is not the same

As tin say or a postcard

Mending Wall

Frost said free verse is like tennis

Without the net, well fuck that poetry's

No game, it's a way of life we are

Calling to each calling hat on heart

Hand on hat, Ideas by any other

Form or phoneme: hill Hell tell

Trail pill till chill feels heels heal

And anything that means you

Take the ch

Language

The language of patriarchy

Is ridiculous Ezra Pound

Couldn't join up the dots

Impossible men fall this

Is the death of political

Language is the wood

(Vertical) timber (horizontal)

The sunshine flat along

The valley floor out this way

Now that fall to no end not as

Saussure meant it, I'm sure.

Timber

The world as it was never known

Is what you make of it, my Danish

Comes with a bomb in it the English

Department the graveyard of Poetry

Need never know the need

To know never as before happily

Ever after a final blow Personification

And Capitalised Abstraction return

The wood for the trees the timbre to timber

Meanwhile

Back to Orpheus' place and the deadline.

Songs fill the World to bursting bursting

From radiators bursting from grass the chord

That is discord played across blue

Radio

I wrote "radiators" when you thought

"Radios" Jack Spicer say it

Again "radios" thank you

Jack Spicer Orpheus was

Heading up the charts

We all have to make choices

Some of them don

Orpheus

The man who mistook his girlfriend for a wife

Exit separately from nowhere *shall we go*

And sit somewhere else. Eurydice was mute.

And all the tricks of a snake she thought.

You appear a strange colour

In the footlights of my heart

You need to check your email and make-up

More often. Life falls out of your body

The memory fainter and fainter the heartless

Ocean beats how it seems from the window

Every minute I think I'll bump into you

Whatever's in your job description

The original came to me like an angel

With the latest fashions in mind

Swing at anchor it has to swing

I kiss your crystal slipper in the story

Words out of the heartless ocean

Orpheus ragged amateurish

The citizen is all we're left to work with

Life falls out of your heart

Less body

Aide-memoire

My mouth the sweet lyre

Like a big flag turned

On its head o sweet

Little book a fragment

That won't impress

The tooth fairies the whole

Work by natural light

Is the hourglass empty

Instance on the tongue

Like a big flag I was told

All this the first

Instant on the tongue it is it is

Twelfth

(Substitute "cloud" for "ocean"

To make it different in

Brackets the condition

Provisional transpose

Diamond to light

Spicer to replace

Pound for word

Thing slightly less

Than = close

Bracket

Rain

It's no good talking about it

You've got to get wet

Compression of words against

A wall dummies crash mark

Out to right and left temple impact

My sanguine angel stroke

My eyes are red not blue white

Pain at random to the light you

Me strike me everyone else between

Squeeze Reality into as tight

A space as possible the capital "R"

Crushed through a thin mouth to "r"

Windows hold it up to equivalence

To equivalence strange images trail

Compression of light smaller vehicle

Snip of

Cube Moves

Each way you look

Interviewed by maybe an unheard voice

Makes a bottle a bottle

Might break in and across might each way

Ten more minutes o get wet why not

That's the place because that's the way it is

So much so my chin's sore and then into the up

Or a shape of one

Pots jugs bottles

Into jars

When it touches the fabric of life

First drop un-lifelike an open

Letter skyward this is how it is this is no edge but a tin

Cup turned away in that for detail

With us now no smaller than

Bet Wit

From the Idea I've a feeling

Any minute now collides enough

For two Simons where's

There's a language we speak

A room is how it's left

Three on the dot

I've a feeling from the Idea

A feather hard to say mirror

Comes under "w"

Shifted a bit

Tee Hee

Indeed. Stuff.

Wet paint into exact space.

Whatever image title or body's the risk

Lips in the eclipse

Has it has "the" has its position

Chair against door.

Things are now

The way things are too fast to notice.

A chequer-board of desire

One red one blue one yellow one four-sided

Figure not that regular either all closed in

Or no such thing exactly in effect mint

The same "a" indefinitely the same body's

Place where bones fit

Side-netting pushing out into life

It hesitates

Heaps

You walked sing-song to the shape not who

You think it is though

A closing movement in the way of looking

Budge in the other direction makes a note make

A note tipped with your sour kiss as collusion

As collision leaves a signature dissolved to

The next disclosure that's settled then

All traffic stopped next

To the ticket kiosk except blue cars the rest drive on

Air steady film a kind of flame flies through

The coffee table to form thought

A letter I'm writing to someone else. Or this

You wouldn't know. End with a little biog

Or a hard-boiled egg.

Of

Breathless peering at the LCD

Sign after sign after sign after sign

Shake. Tremble. Michelle made up

Surveillance and vertigo echoed

Echo sense after a while

It falls

Horizontal stripes strips also left

Eyes enough to say yes white

Synapse like this little silver whatever

You're thinking no question but it looks

Like one stop call a white "you" printed

Across my red tee-shirt in arial

But we don't we shake

Tremble not so much sense

Echoes up here with the satellites

Language is not optional as you pop we fit

A suitcase into a rubber mat a birdie

What really happened

Slips Light

A white "**YOU**" printed across my red tee-shirt in arial

Parked car then what

Do you think rushes here fits

There the message stops

How it then adds Michelle

Day One

Walked straight

Into sound

Reflecting wave how to use it pull

Anything from your pocket anything

I'll guess right and it'll stick there

Michelle too

Into a sentence sign after

Sign after sign the cloud is

Like a white wing is like a white

Cloud and will it won't parked

Car same day same cloud

As Michelle says

Puts You in the Picture

The index behind always leads to white knuckles and poor
    reflection

If you need more evidence come out with what you see

A white "**YOU**" printed across my red tee-shirt in arial

Flipped completely when Michelle goes you go early evening sun
    mid-September

Polyester Cotton Mix

I see it in all like stripes

Stop start stop

Start stop

Start moving pictures of still objects

Surveillance in the absence of God

Retreat into the body Michelle left

Soft deft a blank rush hour

Get it where it fell

Strips you also of the red tee-shirt

Who's Whose

Echo. Sense of it carries back as a "hello".

More polish. What we want. More spit.

For which there is no evidence. Me peering back

Steer by other stars. What's that buzzing noise?

Stop it. It's irritating. Spicer's listening in. For which

There is none. Not a mirror. Not a moon.

Not an understanding. Funny little thing.

Everyone knows everyone in this explanation.

Goodbye with your heel. Echo the go.

Reality

Doesn't always end up in the same place

Not always where were we

Sparkling where we were language is

Not optional as you pop it in your mouth

People wear stupid shoes in reality. Or Lego.

Rules finish with my heart and give me backache

A doorway sped toward

Ahem Michelle constructed out of surveillance and vertigo

I mean video

Walk towards me and I'm not there

Consistent with water damage

Worked out on ruled paper and too much

To carry Michelle signifies "made up"

Reality is a note

Warm Rain

Let's play with things I think about when you went keep going

Infinity is roly-poly with Death at the end of it not a detail

Missed hot wet new dark

Marks where a chair scraped the grey snow-bright wall

Then off a cliff is knowing where to stop "thank you" in chorus
    is

To throw it away leave it to me sit tight as square is to sway more

Unstable not less

People don't think in sentences people think in puffa jackets

My gaze is a notebook my gaze is an email sick of now not

Taking "things" in

Who's in who's out who's paying

Drops over off out up and that's what

Over the Page

Not a cloud. Like that. Very like that. But not

Suddenly time accelerated and I was gone

No feeling in my legs pearl sky few

Moments after silver

Air the way ice shrivels before heat the chill

Should be here now but I won't go

Orders continue to be issued

"It" says more than we believe we believe

The air that clouds the trees

Was the way but goes nowhere

Not given in a smiley way

Ideas side on

Solution: walk faster. Quick.

Gum Spots

News. Potato. Wedge. Every. Little. Echo

Side on

To think in sentences they think in

Make Ideas all year round with a Big "I" for the minute

Eurydice kept popping back for a good look thick as sentences

To play with Ideas but only play with them coat the floor

With them Time for a good tidy up and Infinity's such a complex
    thing in warm rain in cold

It is quite the news or the echo the chair

Rubbed along the kitchen wall to think in the sentences they
    think in

"Thank you" in chorus

Orpheus with this don't-give-a-damn attitude still cold

Pudge rhymes with judge so you know side

On what stop leaving at the right

Side who's in who's out who's paying

Who sneaks about

Through the elbow knowing when

To

Follows warning

Glance over knowing what pivot

Light not for a minute

Box. Cross. Dot. Mug. Stops.

Lone Star

Whatever you're thinking. No. Not

A question it looks like Michelle

But wraps one way sound

Kind of a shield

Puzzle

As no question is a tea stain

I'm coming to the surface

Sleeping lightly how it fits. Twang

Is a place while it is breaking

Points into sound

And walks towards me

Now

One way to stop. Stop.

And that and flavoured water

Pink usually represents black

Currant through natural light

Keyed in the sky

Blue wall normally sweet we don't want that do we we've got
    this

Says so to the air

Still who says it's not fast but sails away

Dipping

Still warm

Air-Shaped

New Day

Hunt the blossoms in silver after signs first

They don't first places go

Up walk about if it doesn't walk what about you do as you

They don't that's the way signs do

It's the sign

Just Started

Might go wrong. Sounds like you know but at what message

My guess forming the complete picture

Not sure what Friday is for though but it's a one

Off standing next to things

Darker is to see the one-off

Artifact we start with the same material

End up you and you end

Finishing Touch

David are you able. I'm having trouble with. You don't want.

To be someone. Else like the next

Instant air-shaped you

Remind me you

Are audience fragile walk through a new place

Golden light on golden shoulders

I love these afternoon meetings snap finger and thumb heighten
the level thin

Thin just thin

Cobalt

Triangulation point the body enters thingness

Little light through the silver blind

Eyes washed out by daylight

Low lit evening warm and drying

Air warm and silver drying little washed

Same Chair

As a letter acts the repository of the immediate

Comfy

Budge up. Warm evening and a Lloyd Loom dark duck-egg wicker
 is what

What is going on in the street precisely as the cat flea transfers
 its affections to my left

Ankle. Blue plastic carrier brought down by blue rain patterns
 drenched blue

Light drenched street to blue T-Junction the next immediate
 blue

That's turning

Easy Air

Same thing as a red roof tile

Light switched on

In the shed day lit

The grey panelled Citröen van next

Door same chair as a letter

Immediate is the matter

A repository

White drawn on a diamond

Noir

Five seconds away rain look

At it wet mist have a good look precisely over the dot of the "I" or
that grey

Hill the length of the track there

Limits it's what's happening this late Friday afternoon the eyes
of Pallas Athene crystal

Diamond or grey pigeons' wings flutter black and white t.v. light
and not so light a film

Precisely over a dark lake swerves in and out rain comes down in
focus light forced out

Under the iris

Experienced rough scratchings

Out logged call as "are" and "the"

Cold Lake

Swerve in and out rain comes down

Coat

The idea is. Would be okay tells you what impermanent light
    under cold

Iris is it

It is not dropped like the one's that followed

And the not

So good cobalt to chemical

Off-grey and grey pigeons black and air-shaped seems there
    are no

Advantageous Thing

White quickly became the idea it would be

Okay tell you what the iris it is not anybody's flutter but and
    only the one's that followed

Smell

Nice music floating from the house to warmer

Fingers new scrubbed with cold tap water

And detergent

Baltic White

On the line of morning possibly flattened out

Reading the map one step over from the idea

Of Capitalism leaves no choice or room for now

Suppose all the pixels fell out

That'd be fun

The Ideas the map why do

Why Do

Dry stones

Disappoint wet stones

Inspire no excite they can they do I'm not trying anything clever

Polished stones from the beach you know

Iced Water

I really need a glass of red

Would tap water do no

More than history piling up behind

Windows and quarter-lights before

Paper Clips

Drop them and they fall into new

Shiny chill and air never enough

Write it on my hand the tight I almost fold

Like the idea windows to give some aside

Lemon chin

Direct Light

Tight reflection I almost go into and calm down

Now I've got the whole of Western Civilization

Pressed behind me surplus to pixels and dormer windows

Brighter when open

To air or scissors

Leave the tip one

Dot

One on icon

Lost only to itself you

Mirror behind disappears

Starts to tip and list lisp twist by

Sunlit where that does

You or me sweep end on a

Soup

Green plastic washing line—how many things can a head hold
    so that's

What's it's like glass

Half veer

Away elbow wet no harm only slightly

Worse the entire bag though which

Way was

Which full-pelt through air

Thin new bubble let me put it

And there's your answer orbit

"Orbit" I jotted down and so up it pops as soup

Else like the next instant air-shaped thin as the next as thin as

Thin as and as clear as chicken soup

That's what's it's like that thin

Air Thin

Next stress and remember darting

A few quid knots one millimeter else like

The next fragile walk through a new place

Blue Felt

Blue felt comes out of blue felt

Is the one to think I remember I was

Veneered draw bangs shut

So we could arrive about two thirty

Sometimes the light will bend back the lemon

Its brighter peel

Utopia Station

Shuts the drop use the lemon

Back and back and back

Video Black

I walked to Hayley's but it could be Hades

The eyes were taking notes

Complete sense out of sight

Earplugs in this head

You can see clouds let them dissolve jump

Inside how the unmarked tallies with lillies lillies with stars

(Spotlights) in the firmament (ceiling)

jump inside the Sublime then jump

The eyes dart dark then gone the present goes

Crashing past the left

Ear let

It dissolve

Cream to white white to white above to China Clay what wheel
    what sparrows' reply

(Cheep cheep) as fibre-board sits one of those jump-off-

The-cliff empirical certainties to melt lettuce

The light will

Bend back its brighter peel to sublime fault fold on

Sub e f d

Chinks

Where things don't but doors did.

Tie down orange =

Fire where

Flare = strike where red

Means boss and black

Equal to variable and magenta

= lemon broken

Paint and broken wood clouds

Translucent upstairs' windows

hanging from take

The air hinged raw

Data box

Ticked like me

USE BLACK INK PLEASE it says

It always says that bit in black ink

Flip-flop

White sound sand surf coast

Line. Ache behind the eyes

For this scene at least yes

We're by the sea then

Wholeness rolls who knows

From that angle light-heartedness

From the bottom whatever you think up

I scare below scar in sight

That image resembles the one I said

Senseless reflection to the next reflection senseless

Imagine the unimaginable Infinite

Summer air what "it" was is gone

Drops to the floor

"+"

Clearly

Is is clearly the relation to cross-hatchings to double beat to Isis
    to two is's

Skin in to touch

Alone absence is out

Present the present grows

O files brimming emails o grey o downpour o lost

Opportunities flailing arms dash along the road prescient as
    Tweedledee

They are arriving in taxis daily as bygones trickle past

Moonlight above Hartley's crib all of a muddle sunbeams and
    rain lifts up

Down your absence is o air

A rose a rose a rose a rose a rose a rose

Is your presence Tweedledum

Subsidence trickles grey and cold to subsidise to subside

Downhill is easy and easier no losers think whichever

Instant exclamation marks prescience on the instant o

Zero O

Fizz

That's what—no exclamation marks for you my boy as grey is
    cold and of white

Ceiling above a thin stain

Sky cleared of satin light where the sound is skylarks

Up and down all day long fills the absent eye blocked open hazel

Green as a marble the idea the area small sample a speck

Caught sunbeams as muddled as rain

When the sound paper cups blow about

Bite through Reason if I can just pull it apart

As soon as field is to sky yellow is to white

Counts the sound o to stop it up where it is

On the instant

On the Instant

Where is the sound you can't open

The idea I suppose bit through at the "e"

Pull it away one clean white sheet like summer

Mirror to the alias wipes it out no single moment

Life is grey

Horoscopes are upbeat

Towels are delivered with tongs

Behaviour is inappropriate if we don't know

Where it leads write it out and wait

Summer with ice

Tap the glass. Hi.

First Aid Box

You you you and you in this instance

First mirrors then coat pegs where we are in this sentence

No single one alias my mirror first mirrors first maybe we do
    maybe

We don't don't we make lists seep edges

[Unfinished]

And there's more.

Black and white stopped like a photograph

Shifting furniture about for the nth time today then lights out

Drifting off over the fence and away where the eye can't settle

Rain streaking grey laminated panes float in the orange clouds

Rain

Persists. Turning inward to the white mug

And scrubbed kitchen table dyed midnight

Blue changes as autumn weather or Dot's latest mood

Angels black I didn't do it I didn't do it but you did

Thump

This is one of my poems that starts serious and high

Then tails off. Do we have a story or a plan?

Do we have a story then? So up it pops as soup

Soap. Breathe overall finish with a sign

Like a sign a dead body away from this side on this

Occasion finish with

Side to Side

Cloud spinning wedged open

Nice sunny day cipher missing

Top left

Off hands open the thought of you

It's away beyond the flap of windscreen wipers

Cries

Lead out to hillsides obviously light

Barely drumming the table grey detail caught

Glimpsed frozen angel white flashes under wing

Agree

Or not. Ten minutes to

Silver echo which way they think which

Ever note that's left

Image

Leave it in the window

Lead out then tail off

Rain

Persists angels black with missed

Communications rain falling grey

Does it matter if one follows

The other arranged along one line

Square One

WIDER & WIDER

The air is blunt and soft

Hammered concepts

Until they fell apart

Lone damp jackdaw flops down

BIN LINER

Lone damp jackdaw flaps across

AIR STRIP

Lone damp jackdaw touches down

Then off that's the first sign

The air is blunt and soft

Fib

First sign's first freeze the frame

Ten minutes falling into my grave

Falling under falling eyes

Sunken or broken

Zap Bam Pow

Give a false name where I am

In relation to the good there's a light on in the room. I am not
    alone.

We are happy. The idea is the first time to make a note. Drop in
    the fresh

Air leaves drop grey walls of cloud manufactured warm shade

But there are no meetings scheduled point-blank

The air is blunt and soft push me in the right direction fell apart

I grow wider and wider and wider and wider and wider and

Squared we were little dots

Air

First name "crunch" second name "mess"

Whatever attaches as stars wheel over nightly

Air chiseled from rock laughter echoed

Wind gets up breezes freshen distance away over

Fields touch of chrome yellow neat cut off point

Dead Spot

A line through it and my eyes

Person first mirror second

Tighten butterfly nut follow

Instructions to the let

Me sharpen my pencil nothing disturbs

The air

Pale

Go to the park and climb a tree

Acid green with ice

Air with ice a storm falls

To regular beats look

At this pool in the new

Sunshine

New Management

Well I'm scratching my head why aren't you

The white motorboat draws full circle

Dreams lost

Conflict lost contact

Olive-skinned I leap over the trail

Nothing disturbs the air thin enough

Tipped with blue

Cypress trees at the door

Whichever

Tipped into sky and loosen clothing more to remember

The experience than the reference at odd

As your tongue does it an alternative metaphor for "like" please,

Let's see the idea would

Be okay if it existed and there were bubbles

Left add more and add how the world fits

Think bottom top to left lift to

The surface seconds later slow or low

Finish Off

Coast, coats which is what

You see in the carpet

Figurines marching to look

Upon the same emulsion ceiling cream as beige

Paper cups blow about but no they are white

Shockingly *there* in a line

With a line through it

More to remember

If I can just put it right

Here the World will flow

Waste Ground

Sunlight dropped on black

Funnels young birds intent to look one is winter one is summer

Can't be wrong

Time of year dash dot dot dot

In the cards hearts of course bleaker

Blacker is the measure of

Pretty lost join the procession through

The edge

Do with your mouth whatever there is to do

With your mouth loss is error sit and watch

Without realizing it united untied is a way of reading and
      missing a go

Only the ocean this occasion

In Reality

An appointment book with a black cover machine-stamped
    "2004" inscribed in gold

The dreams that die in small children's eyes shining snow

Black and white "still" colour on the video "hiya" starts off

Where we left it at the stair's foot

"Now" too quick to record whatever you do with your mouth

Off We Go

Valid one day next day the newsagent must not be considered
    the serious thinker

The post requires anchoring with nylon cord beyond that I'm not
    telling

When actually I don't know if we can write these things at the
    same time

It seems we can six months in which brings me to

Soundtrack

Flags are limp and wet the hair like fishbones there's a smile for
    you we can write these things

Down into a kind of memory beyond the limit it was the kind of
    daft

Dead-pan realism received into dream shadows passing even

Note

A story about this is one side in some ways just a note

As If

Big red ugly pen to the echo of straight through

Ocean extinct ocean next to it straight light

Water days mostly I refuse

Boughs

Drive up and under park I don't know what to do from here

As the cold air hits you plenty of tables to fill and theories

To fill them with I hardly know you when likes and dislikes

Are the same thing leaning the voice against a rising shower

Sweet and clean lightning rushes home

Warm

Despite the displacement of twenty-four hours

Despite the displacement of twenty-four hour traffic

Which makes this more anecdotal not less like a rubber ball

The references checked out face half

In light

Crossings Out

I'll shift my position if I want to

Oh yes, eyes straight ahead

Keep things factual and many weathers

Partly gleaming

Nothing But

Half light half nothing like more like more nothing

Green mug on the green rug

Face in Light

And the chrome handrail tips your image left

Leaves twist through frozen air which sounds sound

Now pure now white now now

Traadaa

Light blooms and wet concrete dries pure and grey

And I promise I'll concentrate more fully on what you're saying.

Snug in my footprint. Sweets and bumpf too.

Oh, Yes

Voice. Carry. Get up. Disappear.

There the pulse ends. It was a bad moment.

The red team loses.

Despite this setback I got out of the car and walked towards the
stairs face half

Cloud

Beauty is there in the same breath trimmed to a new minute

Of stars of feathers or sharp gum Beauty is a minute

The Real is a metaphor for

Streams of the personal need not trouble us

Within days or even a synapse clicked fingers

Throw the top after the empty bottle

Who's is the white face echoing T.V.

Where we start is where we go

Seize that expression one step ahead where the door is
    misreading is

Part of the job

Red comes to mind then fades

More responsibility in the grey rain. And then more.

Slip Ons

Where Ideas get you is clearly the wrong choice.

The sky fades and is pink

A key question for nice people like you.

The key is not fuzzy otherwise it's not a key.

The present was soon exhausted. Is, was.

Chocolate, a teddy bear (for children). A ring.

I got word through the mail but I'm happy I've found hard to
    understand

But respect those who do and those who don't

You have to to make it right

I should be using a projector not paper

Eyes those eyes more real than the Real

The sky's still here and pink not faded

So the statement is untrue

"The sky fades and is pink"

And bets are off is true as a statement as I can mean

The word "montage" (just the word)

Fills me with terror

Like, "we took him to one side" in the pub fills me with

The tide went out then the narrative continues.

Wow

When Muses feel abused nothing courses through break of
    reflection

Not this one. Not this. Not

Why the change of shape immediate arrow thin in air shaped
    with light

Wander in gentle grey morning light but he doesn't know yet

Notes, notes, notes. More notes. Voices carrying families, dog-
    walkers, tourists

Centre to the immediate under a thin coat heavy rain pelted the
    office windows grey air

A long red squiggle, red squiggle, long red squiggle

"Mercury" chalked in yellow where dust particles bounce on or
    off the grey pavement

Cold and real memory is made from the optic nerve feeling not
    much but the shine

In all directions

Spring

And a stabbing pain

Memory as a form of concealment as a memory

Force it out it's a Thursday so you can relax now cut

In the immediate you cut to

Ask for to write up and finish the book so much depends on

The handwriting by the left-hand margin usually pink and ruled

Usually pink as the evening sky or some other cheap metaphor
    for metaphor

Or titillation, smarty pants and words don't do all the jobs
    they're supposed to either

And as usual the usual disappointments

Usually disappoint no matter how much you repeat "usual"

Surrounding Areas

The layer perhaps brown light-grey

Charcoal sandwiches of pure line

Lines of gravitational pull there and between

To feel satisfied or good as that blue wall

And seems right for a cloudless sky

There is every reason to feel

Satisfied present and present identical the two

Split moments and movements inseparable start

With the intellect move backwards

Or start with the body same method or trajectory

Silently falling a voice converted to little bits

Hot or miss or guess a summer wash

Vert a shade holds to a shade a context

Thick

Like a truck empty driverless truck indicating left well not quite

The secret of forgetting proceeds without reference

Guess or stay silent what you might

Until today dead rooftops of this city

Roof after roof after roof

Your proposals taking the air

The details close the story or what's waiting

Round the corner

The round brown pot containing loose tea

My offer to cook fore-grounding a white enameled stove

Bought outright the minute

Look back where accidents clustered to explain

The theory and whatever's true brightens later on

Solid State

Off to one bite down like flattened piano music

Bottled water whilst taking air packaging informs

Usefully there are 20 secrets and volume control

Is one of them as these are 19 gleaming locks

No wear or tear

Nothing beyond gleaming gleaming beyond nothing

Okay then

Quiet Breeze

A moment and a theory slide down air do not appear

But a tulip tree and its lush green leaves with a stopper

Comes next more ink than sense without the axe cropped

Landscape arrives in details need bother us like their cold

Air clouds fluffy as potato lifted with my fork eyes hard

Up to the light which brightens as seen from a slit trench

Later: (a) that minute (b) accidents (c) bottled water (d) industry.

An Illustrious Record

On a long day choosing footwear then home

Blue clouds invisible to the memory

Don't like this don't like that but clean and sharp

Where I'm up to in a sense of my happiness

Lets you off the hook ajar a little way open or a cow

In the next poem a china pig hopping over the moon

Err Um

So we do what

Chess or cheese takes a sip drops a soft

Low table a spot I can't think with

The weak light of the low inhospitable sun

Move off the off-beat I wait part fade

Part of the name sits here to barely touch bottom right

Hand

Choice

Never trust a man who won't take his coat off

Images turned to rubbish by metaphor

Beauty slows down to a stop

Never quite the answer it is

About a year later

Managers sit down and stand up

Look-who's-reading-in-my-front-room

Daddy bear took the golden top once

Over the top come my eyes into that face

Warm outside the radiators flushed to max

Tick the moment where it lies

We live one beautiful afternoon floods the next

Collect stamps with no questions

Melted Paper

Today blue signifies distance and nothing else

What does "gel" do

Down like rain or fulfilment

Touch is a degree of brightness

Lick the days clean if you're a cat

Like normal people doors are squeaky birds

And this is my "cat poem" dreaming cars

"a" + "b" = "c" and you follow the same path home

Cow

Icky is sticky and other such tropes/metaphors/synesthesia

Consciousness or what you call work weren't made to wear shoes

Like that voice you insisted on

If you can hear through speakers and look at paintwork

Forward

The jolly cash machines dance past

Bubbles rise to the surface a few yards off

I recommend back out through where evidence shows up green

Then take a brick called "take" with clouds in it

Cold

Cowed is the issue vertebrae played like a harmonica

Incompleteness is a view we can set aside now the meal is ready

Can't get the images out quickly enough or a swipe card

A tram or term or tern or turn or tune or telegram

The same music through water pressing forward to glass

Another Big Day

Silver cover translates as silver clover

Same music the air so thick I'm swimming through you

Eyes caught on the white flowers of the blackthorn or brambles

Could be brambles and my cells locked in me forever and no
     further

Big Day

Somebody put the light on break with the cloud

Jesus seemed a sociable fellow texting furiously

To hit you on the moment or amoeba

Touch the red green or blue wire meaning distance

Money comes with a wallet

Still in charge of the afternoon off then Infinity

Impedes progress and all you say is true

Grey, in Theory

Old Ticket

The blue and brown book dated **10 DEC 1999**

Archway spread with all its golden northern light

Head back to then and I should cry for a year

It's down the hill to where two are

And let's rely on that feeling or a lark's

Bone-thin and mistaken for paper

Besides which silver rails will gleam far and infinitely

Neat people don't like brains we're down to

One or two inhabitable moments as clouds fluff up

Where the City spread below consciousness

Dirty paper and bags blown skywards by those who buy the
    world from where they are

Exiled from complexity we feel nothing but live here

Suffer a seamless coinage or treat

The rest wake up to beside no need

Happy Dish

What was that voice flying out to where skylarks sing and that

Last little bit of heavy industry right of the disused yard

Air is the ghost touch and irrational light chips at my flesh

The safety glass precisely what it says it says

A cut off point for the saying in kit form

People that matter turn up and make hand signals

Jump out at you and ask have clouds been formed

Differently for the last 40 odd years make a connection

Fit for another place or flit through the unseen meadow

Which could be our good health if bluebells were seen

For their worth within uninhabitable moments to come

Locate the speed cameras that should do the trick

Then relax hands burn for a few seconds immersed

In bargaining what "we" and therefore you want

Make up conversations and the connection is all we ask

Coup

Fill a cup of tea with tea I lived through the 80s

And it was no good **L**   **I**   **F**   **E**   cascaded out of my head

But first a mug and it's the people matter

There you are sitting at the pine table writing

Notes shopping lists and letters on leaves for leaving

Take a sip

The chicken disguised as a cheap joke creeps in to scratch the
     surface

You swim down a map for the future that never comes

Brush into the cup what's done and is best alone

Of accurate report

Orange

Piles of apples and lemons awkward dim and slow

Scents ascend the air to the valid point

Like sun spots sans sense and other celestial punctuation

Inserted between piles of yellow clutter (light)

Are these grey socks yours or mine? Culture sticks in the grey

Of an evening in and white noise trips other sorry moments of
reference

Sub Station

Inserted between clutter and culture the horizon's yellow rim

Living in a swamp of useless bric-a-brac unconnected

Utensils books a toy truck with nearside rear wheel missing

CD without a case. The wallpaper is green or cream and it fills
    my days

Notebooks for miles and miles before and behind glitter

I lean forward and walk the straight line to the loss

Of balance. There is a song in the body. At least three.

Echo Round

I fly about the room and upset people

And the dials you're the magician

A second ago you're not

I'm talking to a star I'm talking to a twinkle

Did so with a sense of we've-been-here-done-this-before thought
    process

Like the knowing how to put one foot I've forgotten to the
    approximate here

And your body a look adored before light

Accelerated to visibility

Where you are no longer where you say you are eyes ahead

Now you've arrived

A pin-prick enters this pinhole camera of a Universe

The sphere tuned to the radio and you're gone in clouds of
    analysis

It's that kind of know how now inhabits those spaces

Know that the word is "napkin" for napkin

Thumb in the dyke forms one alternative or choice

Promises are a kind of trick that keeps coming true

Simon

These poems ought to be written like sonnets on a blinding
    napkin

That's the word — "napkin"

The word for napkin is twinkle or timetable. The choice is God.

We see the truth without waiver or falling over in those spaces
    they spoke

The Idea of choice curses the land of speech

Choice

Spooks only wear white I surmise

Pass the other wall a shadow

That's their choice without

Waving because they have no hands or arms

So they can't open the window or door but float

Through like cats

Cats are spooks

Both seem to possess no manners

But scratch at a window like real cats who starve

For a let's face it an indifferent plate of meat in gravy and
    biscuits

Oh don't forget the biscuits

Biscuits the best bit or to escape the downpour

So much so I pull the Idea of choice up by the scruff

A curse for man and beast (in this case history a cat)

Choice and spooks are a sheet

Inhabit the same Universe but the sheets

Over my head the stars made from holes

In that image we reach the land of forgetting

And the dead filed along the field

Promises are a kind of choice

Where the curse is a trick when partly

We are the absent star

Boxed outside the skylight

Thin Air

When they fall children are the cards in order

A pattern we can't trace it is not chance purely they fall in

A kind of trick that comes true not to be broken

Starlight   starlit   star

White

Colours too bright to name any

Cards work in any order

A pattern we can't trace when it's not

A chance it's pure or as they fall

Holes in the blanket or sheet

Not stars but pinholes

Held the light

Through black cotton

Acrobats

When the children return we will go to the circus

I promise big lights big colours especially red

Okay add green if you want. And tricks. I promise.

Promises and tricks

White

Nice in off

Is As

The sky and horizon record blue Infinity close by the brown roof
    tiles of my parents' house.

Always have always will.

It landed there with it's capital "I" and never melted,
Never went away, a clean and dense snowfall the year 1978.

My mother arrives safe as an ironing board.

She walks across the street in front of the mini-mart and is gone.

My dreaming starts, and that is as strong a proof as I know.

Writing

Black and white jumps focus

The same moment it saves my life

The afternoon is strangely grey

Saves my life for another five pence extra

Promises are a kind of trick that comes true

Shiny Beach

What happens next

Tell me God held a ball of flame held behind a naughty child

And a child's green beach ball tops the list of greenness of all
    the greennesses

Lime juice peas warm sea garden chairs and table large umbrella
    spinach

That's my list started now jot down yours

The shiny white bath I'm lying in is plastic

Easier to fill enamel I prefer though colder

Constellation

Cello and cellar

They don't know and I don't

A black hole would make good a necklace of significances

May be consolations remembrances they are the stars

To Moment

This elastic thing of my life

Talks out of a feather

I know not now a look

It's the way things come out attached

By the rope of the guts and who pays for the salad

I do we all do and we drink an ocean

To sink to the bottom of it

Two minutes past two by the lit match

Silvers to rain

The whoosh of traffic kind of bounced

A strange orange streak pinky sky lays

Over a chalked horizon

What November 8th is a sign marches down

To the whole salad and nothing but the salad

This means it will never stop the detail pin

Sharp the miracle I wanted to believe the trick I wanted to twist

Freezing tap-water

Hands beneath and that is that

Moulding this side to this membrane

Rubbing a feather off **[clap]** **[clap]**

Cloud

Float about and then what

Wood-formed concrete about eye-level

That's what a room above visible

Leaves a shadow left by the dark cloud

Traffic whoosh crosses the river

Khaki troop carriers 1,2 and 3

Strange days these

Pfuff

Into the glass the sunset and its long arm

Raindrops dissolve low visibility equals grey light

Like my eyes like yours and other reference points

The playing card is the traffic island

Borderline salad/garnish/salad/salary/wages

The four of hearts and a salad

Every lining has a silver cloud

A cold blind day a winter's day

Her name was Stella

Theseus' Dad

Black sail, white sail light wing as easterlies drop canvas

Billows light as light Aegeus reaches out for silence

Surveillance Camera

I'm stuck in the book of joined up thought

Fine shoulder-length hair

I've plumped up the velveteen cushions

For the sense sense of occasion

Michelle crosses the zebra

These last unnumbered colours dissolve

Switch on the tap and let it run

Units of light a truck is a kind of articulated trick

The 15 second movie clip

Pin-sharp spreads the spectrum

Black is not blank but grey is his hiss

Complex complex as salad the unit of thought

The other side and "YOU" if you are next

Run-off as raindrops dissolve to coalesce

Grey light for two minutes

Strip-lights puffy clouds tower blocks Infinity Truth

The Universal Man the blank pages of attendant horror

Shoulder to the image if you want to grow up and be a big fly

Formal Solutions

How many body parts tickle at once

There is no getting away from detail

Feet drawn under shade

Seagulls touch fences then think

Better to offer an example

Blue raven's wing of a sky further

Proof for no good reason finger

Tips and needles through

Michelle tippy toed opposite

Thought through

Thought so thought

About thought once

A Harsh Light

Ideas held together with tape

Branches leaves underneath

Tight on detail long on ideas

Trees exhale a million million

Ways not to think or reflect

Simply rain pouring simply

By calm blue lakes beside

Calm blue hills on calm blue

Days a wisp up here air

Borne momentarily simple

Library pictures sharp colour

Sings away behind the eyes

Ideas no one sharper universal

Than the Michelle I knew hazy

As distant as others as ideas

Michelle

Bright afternoon walk her data on file

Then just when it's been a quiet week

Energy efficient calm helps

Seeing her double she keeps busy

Talking between quotation marks

A breezy freshening up her talk

All talk stops to thinking but not

The feeling she busies in the good

Measured crank of 35mm sloping the while then

When her red tee-shirt undoes "YOU"

Never knew love before you say

Where real feeling is focused

Digital today then gone

Just then

Masks the sun-swamped days to come

Those Days

Reduced thought with a bump

The slope when nothing the active focus

Michelle had one once wind of

Vinegar to wine as sky is

Clouds passing the information look like

The information they look like

The following report people spoke amongst them

By which comes close you're left

Neat of course no landscape but dotted

Fence posts downwind

An anchor of stars shattered light

Once mine now below busy stuff

Follows up shaved light in the air

Above the beach-

Silver Coins

Grey light burning paper and rain at the end

Pure gold when echo finds you where echo

Finds you. Does he look like you would she?

Too many "I"'s for comfort

Or "O"'s sparkle over the line and spill

Three-quarter view smear blood over pink

Flesh whatever is invisible is merely flat

Is ocean invisible engulfed? Could be.

Dear

Shut up and stop thinking about it

Believe everything shaky and swerve

I am in every shining thing

I am the shoe-shine boy

Story So Far

Little too much

One green wave then one green wave

The Good Bit

Arrows

Light seeps beneath cloth

Virtual children climb about

The virtual climbing frame

Fall off

Lend me that quality that I should look

We want to know

Theory becomes habituation and grey as paint

At any point what is right always will

Eyes opening to the bloody spot

Realism

Digital opening eyes to net curtains with no connection grey
　　blur or smudge and I look

Made

Throw your heart not in it wave crash I can hear you saying

What we are for this experience and drop off the edge there we

Copy

Dissent in all its metamorphic forms

Skyward crash down where light fades into paper

Families die so we live

Trip backwards the wavey heat

God came along and ate the World

Where are poetry and ideas where's the thread

A descent in a bucket

Community shone a soft pencil

Light drawn in switched electricity

Foreign dams or where oilfields appear end

Less truth till the heart I'm not interested in

The purity I'm not interested in the twist

But nails painted a cellulose baby

Pink squeeze the truth from finger tips so the heart tastes sweet

The purity I'm not interested in collects

This in the grey light and love in the shape of

Flit

Easy smile

Love in the shape

Put there and gone

Hum

Love in the shape of

But I don't know the words put and gone

Like remember '73 or '98 for a nice evening walk

Same thing squeeze the truth till the heart pumps sweet

Human and walking held to the shoulder like an AK47

One remove but wrong delivery fell to my hand

A pulse of green back of the retina plush lawns and plush lawns
        plush lawns

One Remove

All-seeing eye the impossible I'll start with

And the shortest distance then maybe glass

What I do know is

Made

Throw your heart into it

Wave crash I can hear

You saying when we are for this experience and drop off the
edge there we

Structureless

This is maybe the wrong order

Pull the arrows out

Chew

See to it

Brush down straighten sleeves

Film

Human moving human moving human

Moving human moving human moving

Printed in the United Kingdom
by Lightning Source UK Ltd.
120635UK00001B/448-456

9 781844 712540